WINTER WHEAT

David Lockwood

For Mrs H. A. Harris with best wishes from David Lockwood.

GOMER PRESS
1986

First Impression - November 1986

ISBN 0 86383 229 6

All rights reserved. No part of this publication may be reproduced, stored in a retrieval system, or transmitted in any form or by any means, electronic, mechanical, photocopying, recording or otherwise without prior permission from the publishers, Gomer Press, Llandysul, Dyfed.

Printed by J. D. Lewis and Sons Ltd.,
Gomer Press, Llandysul, Dyfed.

For
WILLEKE
who made happiness possible
also
DIANA and LAURA
who helped

CONTENTS

Page

PICTURES
Soon to sleep, ever awake	11
J. M. W. Turner	12
Pre-Raphaelite Analysis	16
Fidelity	18
Macao	20
Weavers	21

OCCURRENCES
Poor Monkey	25
Elkstone and . . .	26
Oxford Station	28
Not really there	29
A Reminder	30
A Skirmish	31
Miles Ignoto	32

A TIME AND TIMES AND HALF A TIME
Winter's Prisoners	35
Come the Spring	36
An Easter: the Easter	37
Re-Union	38

PEOPLE
An Ashram in Eastwood	43
Eve	45
Thomas Carlyle	46
Amelia Opie	47
Cowan Bridge	49

DREAMS
A Dream	53
A Half-dream	54
Gymnopedie	56
Trails	59
The Dance	61

PICTURES

We gaze from bareness and narrowness into the rich outside.
JENS CHRISTIAN JENSEN

SOON TO SLEEP, EVER AWAKE: for Kate Goodwin

A little picture,
a little child.
A small head,
in a bed.
A large pillow,
a sweep of sheet.
A pink bud
beneath a calyx of curls
and eyes that look
and look and look.
A concept caught
to last, outlast
the father who drew
his daughter: also the daughter.
But tells of his love
and the moment
forever.

J. M. W. TURNER

So much, nearly all,
but not quite.
Just as well
or the search might have been abandoned.
The struggle always,
and always a different struggle
was to see as others,
then make others see as you.
Always the struggle
with the evil behind the easel,
his mother,
to be painted out.
'Oh why does love cause so much pain
To wound and gripe the heart and brain?'
Afraid, afraid,
he found his temporary solaces,
odd widows, ugly drudges.

Classical chimeras
and ever the storm.
The vortex,
the seething womb
of dark, of light,
of life, of death.

Suddenly, in Petworth came peace.
Aristocratic plenty
with, strange to say,
culture and comfort
and not the faintest clink of chain.
Happiness that proved
a promontory and a tangent

from which to shoot and stand
and seek detached
the frailty of man:
the puny paddle-blades made
so pointless in the storm.
The turbulence, the confusion,
the contending elements
have a pattern and a passion,
aesthetic, obsessive,
social and sexual.

Dinner in Albemarle Street.
"You'll take down Miss Elizabeth Rigby"
"Some preening pretty miss
either bored, or worse, afraid."
"See, Mr. Turner, the candlelight
upon the spoons
and look at the ceiling."
He looked, it was studded
with lunettes that danced.
"I'm too old for this."
He looked at her again, she looked at him.
Her eyes had a refining fire,
they saw him, his own self.
They did not see
a little man and mean,
even old, still less mad.
Not even an artist
with a capital A.
She did not seem to see a genius.

"She saw me."

"Will you come to my gallery?"
"Say very little, my dear,
he does not like mistakes.
He can be cruel."
"This is one of my best."
She looked and forgot her mother's words.
"Is it the end of the world, Mr. Turner?"
"No it isn't. It's Hannibal crossing the alps".
"So it is, and there's the elephant."
Both laughed and mothers drew further away
from both.
"Too much yellow, Mr. Turner,
Yellow isn't glory, that is white.
Deny it if you can."
He remembered the lunettes
and when the ladies had gone,
as the port was pushed around,
he had looked at the ceiling:
a depleted sky. Just one lunette.

White, white underlaid and over,
Less glory, less fear;
Now a tranquil truth.
She said,
"He can never, never be vulgar,
if vulgar means common;
his faults are as rare and as lovely
as his beauties."

In the low room a candle burned,
beside the bottles and the spoon.
He saw one lunette of light
dancing on the sloping ceiling.
"Elizabeth, Elizabeth, why don't you come?"
She never came, she never knew.

Bartlett and Booth failed to understand.
Lady Eastlake walked a different world,
over a frontier only Turner
permitted himself to cross.

Amidst the elegance came the news
"Turner is dead."
Elizabeth Eastlake wept.
"My dear, it is not the end of the world."
"True, true, but it is the crossing of an alp."
It was the end of a love.
Lady Eastlake became formidable.

PRE-RAPHAELITE ANALYSIS

Holman Hunt could not know,
   But it is so, just so.
In your picture Claudio and Isabella stand
He fidgets chained foot with restless hand.

Some know well, very well, that Hell
   Bound in an unlighted cell;
A sister patient perplexedly kind
Seeks to assuage the lancinating mind.

How did you know, how did you know,
   That it is so, so?

When my soul is mute, mute
   Like Claudio's much be-ribboned lute,
And soft hand is on my heart repelled
Then all love is expelled, expelled.

Often other, then free, free, free,
Even laughter in that prison-yard tree.
And lute off peg is in the hand
and I, too, laugh in no man's land.

Leaves lift and dance in lusty Spring
   Leap to the wind a youthful fling.
They seek no exit like Claudio, chafe and bruise
Twist and curse and always lose.

Lift down the lute, pitch your key,
   The key to your autonomy.
It hangs there upon the wall.
It is all, all, all.

How oddly comforting of Holman Hunt to know
   That I am so, just so.

FIDELITY

The confident girl in the gallery
Stopped before the picture.
"A fine piece of Impressionism,
Beautifully composed, economic with colour.
It also tells a story, the father on the cob
The young couple behind.
'The ride through the Dunes by Mauve'".

Do I, from my grandmother, alone
know of this flash of a tale?

She turned, smiled and gazed,
The old man, her husband,
Ambled ahead.
From her chestnut she looked
At the young and elegant equerry,
Slim contemprary,
Reining in more than his grey hunter
With a supple wrist
A long booted shank
And a manly flank.
He, too, interprets.

They could speak,
This properly caparisoned pair,
The ample ambler ahead
Is deaf, as well.
A moment caught with fidelity,
When male looks at female,
Female looks at male,
It was, they are, beauty.

But the chestnut felt
The slap snap of the crop.
Beauty was outflanked by Duty.

Dust and a flash of a tail.

MACAO: picture on a plate

They stand, they sit, they kneel,
A happy crowd.
Of pleasant peasant people.
A long scroll flutters down,
A semaphore I do not understand.
Away, surfacing the sea,
A happy town protected
By peaked cones of hills.
Distance draws away to empty seas.

It is a world of oriental innocence
Through occidental eyes.
The people never grow, never rise,
Or drift away.
Their hats pagodaed and perched
On lacquered hair never lift,
nothing shifts.
The tout selling his prophylactic
Makes no sales.
They do not need it.
They have knelt for three centuries
And do not heed it.

WEAVERS: for Theo Moorman

A thread is a line
upon which to hang
another thread.
It can be words,
then more words
to form another kind of thread.
Both words and thread
become a warp and weft,
which turn to
texture, tone and colour
giving pain or pleasure.
They give another line.
If some are absent,
it still is significant.

Both communicate
that something granted
somehow
when dreams and desires
become designs.
Both weavers.

OCCURRENCES

An event has happened, upon which it is difficult to speak, and impossible to be silent.

EDMUND BURKE

POOR MONKEY

How can they convert
The pantry to a cage
With perches and a swing
And a cold northern light?

How can they see
The monkey hunched in unhappiness,
A hermit without vocation?
Conscripted.

Communicate, communicate
Your compassion. I do.
"Don't touch, he often bites."

How can they keep him?
The core of the house,
Shrouded in solitude
Whilst they work good works,
Clinics, canteens, community.

How can they say
They love him, as they do?
Bright chat, I know, at sherry
Of "Our dear little monkey."

They can, they do.
Some bear their own burdens,
Probably inefficient, probably indiscreet,
But they do not keep a doppelganger,
Hunched in unhappiness
In a cold northern light.

ELKSTONE AND ...

This March day I travelled there to see
   The angle of the original axial tower,
The graded pilasters of the new, in short, archæology,
   To appraise the vaunted vaultings and their power.

A bullying wind hustled dark clouds
   But sun fell in shafts of clean gold
On boles of beeches in their argent crowds
   Groups curved and carved in the constant breezes' fold.

Stone was the quality of the day
   The woods were contoured to the limestone hills,
Unmoved, unmoving, they had found their living way,
   Were supple, not static, the evillest of ills.

The church stood strong, firm and fast
   The carved beaked birds around the door
Stood ghastly guard to Jesus, Judge, the last,
   A quailing to the conscience at the core.

> *Set for ecclesiology, I sat*
> *and suddenly was blinded*
> *beatifically by a yellow light,*
> *Turner's golden glory,*
> *which on the altar fell.*
> *A light so old,*
> *yet alive with Spring,*
> *as old as the earth's dawning.*
> *It made these stones young.*
> *In this light I see light,*
> *the zig-zags round the chancel arch*
> *are lightning,*

*even lightening
and enlightening.*

I am alight.

*I gaze and can only
perfunctorily peer
at dragon-head stops
and Kilpeckian corbels.*

This glow stays to linger
   So that I see Painswick spire
Not a heavenward pointing finger,
   Better, a widening shaft of yellow fire.

It is light and light.

OXFORD STATION

She dropped his change,
four p of it,
and besought him with a beseeching glance.
"Good God, girl, don't look
at him like that. You'll be his slave."
A minute later she grabbed his cigarettes,
and I saw that life for them
would always be a shadowed game
of Tit-for-tat.
And it would end too suddenly.

NOT REALLY THERE: On Mount Bromo in Java

Three quarters of the world
I am
away from home.
On a volcano's rim,
fingering the sulphurous side of death,
sitting in an apocalypse.
But,
I am,
no further
than Patrick Bronte's study.
For caution bids me say,
I am
in the Martin landscape
on his mantelpiece.
I've climbed a mountain,
but I will not infringe another rim,
the defences of my mind.

A REMINDER

Eagerly, quickly, delicately
The bird descends the tree,
From bough to branch
Scattering diamonds
At every footfall.
Just like a child I knew,
Who ran downstairs
With keen joy
To catch the moment
That would not wait.

She scattered vivid life
At every turn
And so prodigally
It all went.

A SKIRMISH

The spirit wounded child
with new-born confidence,
like winter-wheat in Spring's heat,
growing in the sun,
refused the offer.
He preferred the old train
to the new sports car.
But he had been taught tact,
"You see, I have a return ticket
which would be wasted."
Confident, yes, but embarrassment
twisted his feet
causing a snarl,
"It's also very wasteful to stand
on the sides of your shoes, like that."
Forty years ago.
He remembers the rebuke,
but better, he smiles
as he recalls
the journey in the train,
Alone.

MILES IGNOTO

The historian revisits alps to relive
his particular place in Europe's wars.
Here he drove his ambulance
in a compassionate hide-and-seek.
He sits with his wife;
they eat bread, drink wine
and in this eyrie think easily
of eternity.
Honing music hums, disturbs.
He stirs and, as of old, he seeks
among the boulders and untender stones.
He finds bones worn by wind,
a rib cage tuned to moan
a threnody from a lungless chest.
What need of words
and of what avail?

They cover him.
No man is silent
till earth encloses him,
and even then?
The historian gives a sad,
a joyless shrug.

"A TIME AND TIMES AND HALF A TIME"

"When I think of the nature of time, I know. When I speak of it I cannot say."

ST. AUGUSTINE

WINTER'S PRISONERS

December edges in the rut
In the road
Sharp glass lattice
Constricting like cruel corsetry
In biting laces,
But only cramping its own self.
Beneath that trellis,
This water window, is winter's prisoner.
It has found a way
And flows its own self free.
It forms patterns;
Air against ice,
Fluid faces,
Contracting, contacting
And performing an amoebic
Parthogenesis.
It is also a harmony
Of silent music:
Mutations eloquently mute,
Serene and sustained,
Pristine and virginal.

Crash, a foot,
A diapason of disaster
In a frail cosmos.
One of Shakespeare's bloody boys,
Wanton,
Thudding an ego around.

Beware,
Be aware.

COME THE SPRING

My cat curled on the bed,
is a prelude to action.
The pink tinted inner of the acorn
curved like a foetus,
with a seeking root like an umbilicus,
seen yesterday,
is a prelude to a tree.
The human folded in the womb
is prelude to the moving majesty
of man.
All coiled, waiting
the spring to energy:
all are tip-toe
to be.

The woman curled and cramped
with cancer in her bed,
is that crouch a prelude
to another Spring?
I pray it is not
truly terminal.

AN EASTER: THE EASTER

A Spring day perfectly remembered?
It is often imprecise, a pastiche
Of lambs, daffodils and catkins,
A bit of a birthday card.
But,
I do recall in War, a day,
a time of shared despair,
grey, cold, threatening,
the bruised green of leaves the only colour.
And
I found a nest by the wall
of the returned-to home.
It held all dreams,
life was alive with love.

It means that flint walls
spell for me
a swift impaling happiness.
Like nests they enclose.
Humans need sharp stones
to cut hostility,
to surround release, relief
and in that case, resurrection.

REUNION

Leaving the dinner, the drink
the deft speeches caressing
the surface of other days,
we walked into darkening streets.
A cat crisscrossed her legs
in swift scissors cutting the road.
She flickered like an old film,
do we?

We are united with some thing
of our younger selves,
but with strange additions.
Our hearts once were hungry,
fed now, but with other food.
To some the goal was been by-passed.
We have encountered realities which we never learnt here,
failed to enquire.
The correct question was not formed.
We are so different,
yet the houses gaze with an amazing unconcern
on us who are and are not
what we were.

We are encountering old dreams;
Making acquaintance with the old self,
other selfsame selves.

This is a seam
the speakers did not explore:
it would displace the seemliness
of an ordered celebration.
All revenants, some richer,

some poorer, some sick,
some bright with health.
But
was what is, all written then?
and
will there be no change in the to be?

PEOPLE

I can look with no indifferent eye upon things or persons. Whatever is, is to me a matter of taste or distaste.

CHARLES LAMB

AN ASHRAM IN EASTWOOD

A curious cairn
in the centre of the room:
a table, a cloth
and a large lace mat.
On the mat a bible
and on that
a pot
and in the pot
an aspidistra.

The bible was, to the mother-builder
of this shrine,
her creed.
It was an ensign,
but it was shut
and weighted down to form
a plinth for respectability.

The plant is erect
with its own aspiration
and a slow certain silent life
raising and unrolling a leaf
in alien air.
In the hard cramped earth
the roots creep inquisitively,
half-starved, but still seeking.
These green leaves,
these white roots
were to fuse and form a coitus
with the black printed pages
of the bible below.

For this strange ashram
of sub-fusc new century solemnity
displayed, betrayed
both the hinderings and the hopes of Mrs Lawrence.
It was a foretelling
about her prophet son.
He wedded the words of the book
and the life of the prisoned plant.

There is a smell of fire
around this pile.
Suttee sacrifice?
For in its fusion
there was furnace heat,
when words, nature and ideas
blazed.
They burnt to kill,
to scorch and scar
all those around:
leaving
D. H. dead
but realized.

EVE

The old Worcester woman
in a bolster of a dress
and with slippers aslop
pulled a branch to peer at plums,
if any. It was that kind of summer.
In her other hand
she had a spray of fresh sweet peas
and, of course, a dowdy frond of asparagus.
Suddenly the morning was alight
from the beacon of her white bright hair.
She was Flora, Eve,
the eternal bounteous mother,
in her garden still.
Glorious in faded fecundity.

THOMAS CARLYLE

His face has printed
a mirror image on the tissue
in such proximity for ninety years;
Two firm faces facing.
Neither is untroubled,
but neither knowingly by self,
they think it is the world,
the suffering of man.
There is more, much more
in these pictured prophets
with their sad eyes for messages
to construe for other ears.
Here are the two Carlyles,
the public whisper and
the private shout.

AMELIA OPIE

The walls quivered with colour,
The muslin round the bed shone
Polychrome.
There lay the old Quaker,
Goffered in flouncy white.

She gazed with an amalgam
Of placidity and joy
At her lustres hanging before the winter light.
They splintered silently
Jewelled daggers of dreams.

Primly she wrote
"My prisms are quite in their glory,
Their radiancy brighter than
I have ever seen."
The red, the orange, indigo and blue,
Splashing spectrum decked her room.

It was the colour of her life,
No bounds to love.
Books, men, poetry and art
Had been enfolded in her outspread arms.

She found her man,
She made him great with love.
Now it is the same.
The violet, the yellow and the green,
Flicker, sometimes fuse
Lines of fascination that suddenly fade.

Still great with love,
She runs to God,
But stops to write;
"Surely the mansions of Heaven must be
Draped with colour unparalleled."
Do you see her,
Or do you see an old Friend
Dying in a plain white room?

COWAN BRIDGE: for Charlotte Bronte

Suddenly, over the bridge
Quite ordinary cottages. It is Charlotte's school,
The loathed Lowood.
Here a dear sister dies.
We peer and tip-toe
This hated hallowed ground.
A sibillant roar, a rushing hush
Draws us to the weir,
Past private beans
And someone's greens.
This is Charlotte's
"Raving sound of Leck."

We see a salmon leap.
Did she see such crash
on jagged crags
And see water starred with blood?
It was only momentary.
She would have understood,
This intuitive urge
To race and upward,
To hurl self at rocks
And win,
To create and re-create.

Seeing those flashing sickle scales
stained with gore,
The unveiled strangely veiling
I thought, she, too, ascended
And with much blood
Spitting from splitting lungs,
Sisters', brother's, then her own.

But before God hooked her,
She had spawned.

Tip-toe hushed
And by this raving rush, remember
Instinct and intuition.

DREAMS

We are somewhat more than ourselves in our sleeps.
SIR THOMAS BROWNE

A DREAM

"Put hand over hand" he said,
"Don't let the rod run through
Or you will burn your palm."
So down the aerial mast I came
To the plain. Helpful little man.

The cavalry moved in disjointed strings,
Slackened reins, ambling hooves,
Clouds of dust.
Picturesque manoeuvres in the sun,
The glory of the soldiery.
I took my message from the officer in charge
and left the room.
Outside, again, the little man stood,
I remembered to salute,
After all, he was the Tsar,
This affable and incompetent man,
To whom my heart went out.
"An Englishman", he said, "How nice."
We talked of Windsor and Walton-on-Thames,
and all in the midst of war.

Poor little man,
I knelt before him and on my head
He placed two white and so soft hands.
I needed that blessing as I left.
The field day was over,
It was cold and very competent cruelty, now.

A HALF DREAM

If only there were a communication cord.
Yes, I know that I'm in a first class carriage,
And what is more I have a ticket for it.

My real relief is that the blinds still work,
The people in the corridor will peer in.
I knew perfectly well getting in
At all
Was a calculated risk.
But at that time it did seem
the train would stop somewhere.
But it just goes on and on and on and on.
The scenery is interesting,
But, oh I do wish it would stop.
I want to pick some of those flowers,
Whole fields of cowslips,
Better still rain clouds of spotted fritillaries.
It's those snakesheads I really want,
But just can't reach. This is a big pain.
So you, too, have heard about the restaurant car.
They are short of food.
They raided the luggage van last week.

But, oh I do wish there were a communication cord.
I don't mind whether there's a station, or not,
Especially if there is a field of fritillaries.

How long in this corner seat?
Far longer than I will tell.
It is a waste,
Particularly if there's a crash.

But, oh I do wish there were a communication cord
and a field of fritillaries.

GYMNOPEDIE

My daughter plays Satie.
Flutes sound virginal and blow
A long long Aeolian flow.
Beneath the grove
Silent footsteps fall
Shadows flicker, spot and band
Falling fortuitous between the leaves
On face and forms below.

The rhythm alters
Before an altar
They turn rise
Curve arabesques
Coil and quit.
There is prowess, there is pain.

The black, the white,
The figured vase,
The printed page
Suffuse and smudge
As focus floods.
A pigment impregnates
Spreading like an Eosin selective stain,
To reveal life beneath the white:
A pulse beneath a skin's membrane.

Greece. Greece. A grace given
To a world in need.
A grace given to me
By a dry man
With a drier mind that
crackled beneath
A cat grey thatch of Boetian hair.

A dispatch case lifted
In a lecture room
With an elliptical arm.
Notes opened and smoothed,
With a parabolic hand,
Up and down, up and down,
The rocker of a rocking horse:
It is the only indication of an
Oscillation in a neat articulate mind.

From him I gained
A frame, in which to fit
Sophocles, Homer,
Aristotle, Alexander and Diogenes.
He fed a platonic tumour of comprehension
curbed by the comely,
The proportion and the form.
He taught, never to be content
with form without content.

Sundays, my Hellenic hours,
Whilst hymns were sung,
I sailed to other gods,
Lycurgos and the Darian League,
Pheidias and Freedom.
But all built on a slave's bent back.
I found a wholeness—flawed,
In a dark room of darker maroon.
A window on a mistless
And unmystic world,
Clear, clean and unclouded,
Direct and finely defined.

Poetry, proportion,
Acanthus and metopes.
These I learnt to love and equally appraise.
I saw without altruism,
Yes, yes, you won.

These facts foundered,
Knowledge cracked and crumbled
Unused over a personal chronology.
Until, pawed, pushed,
In no way awed, distantly bored,
In Tutankhamen's tomb,
Re-erected under raining
Bloomsbury skies,
I was seized and horror surged;
The Blake in me burst,
Against this necrotic naivete.
Egypt be damned!

I fled,
It seemed by chance
To an empty hall of Hellenism.
Yes, empty and that false grave
Was maggot full.
Here was movement in a static world
On Elgin's marmoreal frieze.
Praxiteles.
My daughter is still playing Satie.

TRAILS

"Come live with me and be my love."
And willingly we go.
Aroused, unarranged, aware.
Tensions tauten,
Every passion has its counter,
Cross currents ripple.
We make love only by breaking it.
So we follow a trail
From our parents to our parenthood.
All because of the way
A hand in a glove
Held an umbrella.
So life tilts and angles
At infinitessimal things.
Who is guilty?
Not the man,
Not the woman,
Who cannot tell when she held an umbrella.
It was the unbaited trap that caught
The conditioned victim,
By the wrinkle of a glove,
The hump of the ring
Beneath the kid.
Where had he seen it?
Don't ask me,
Don't ask him,
Don't ask her.
Before their time:
Carriages, a dull day
Parasols furled in neat seamed hands.
Fragmented light glinted beneath trees
On the gold and jewelled knob.

Where had he seen it?
Don't ask me,
Don't ask him,
Don't ask her.
But there was the core of all his dreams.

THE DANCE

Beauty said "Let's take hands and dance."
Beauty is like
A knife in the ribs.
It is a threat
And holds you ransom.
It makes its own demands.
I pay.

Beauty is like
A fly walking on a brass scale
That tips the balance.
It is an ascending scale too.
Beauty is
So nearly reasonable,
But never quite.
To the timid,
she holds menaces.

Beauty has many acquaintances,
Few relations
In any sense.
Good taste is
A distant, very distant cousin:
They meet rarely.

Beauty can lead you
Such a dance.